5-MINUTE GUITAR JAMS

Backing Tracks

JAM TRACKS FOR ROCK & BLUES GUITAR

LUKE ZECCHIN

This book is dedicated to all the friends and musicians I've had the privilege of playing with. Thank you for making me better.

Published by **GuitarIQ.com**

Copyedited by Jason Whited

Proofread by Dan Foster

Illustrated by Jasmin Zecchin

The author and publisher have made every effort to ensure the information contained in this book is both relevant and accurate at the time of release. They accept no responsibility for any loss, injury, or inconvenience sustained by any person using this book or the information provided within it.

Contents

Get Your Free Online Bonus Now!

This book comes complete with free online bonus material. We've compiled a companion website to enhance your reading experience. Extras include audio examples, backing tracks, bonus downloads, and more!

Get your free bonus content at: **www.guitariq.com/5mj-bonus**

Preface

Welcome, and thank you for choosing *5-Minute Guitar Jams*.

Often, the way we practice is disconnected from how we actually use the guitar in real-world situations. In what circumstance would someone stand alone in front of an audience, set the metronome going, and proceed to play a variety of scales and technique-building exercises? Who'd pay to listen to that? As necessary as these types of exercises are for our development as musicians, they're never the end goal.

Mastering anything requires practice; that much has always been clear. Unfortunately, the notion of *practice* is often viewed negatively, as if it's some inherently difficult or tedious task. This mindset has far more to do with our approach to learning rather than the *learning* itself. Simply put, practicing guitar should be enjoyable because playing guitar should be enjoyable! The two are inseparable. If there's a split between our enjoyment of playing and our motivation to practice, then perhaps we need to rethink our approach to practicing in the first place.

The concept behind *5-Minute Guitar Jams* is simple. The whole point of learning how to play guitar is to do something *musical* with that skill. The collection of backing tracks that accompany this handbook are aimed at creating a more realistic playing environment for practicing improvisation, scale patterns, and other technical exercises.

The goal of this short guide is to help you get the most from using these backing tracks. This includes taking a detailed look at each of the progressions used and outlining numerous scale options for improvisation. Beyond this, the aim is to help refine your playing skills by becoming more intentional with your practice time. In short, this handbook will encourage a fresh way of thinking about practicing that's both engaging and effective.

I sincerely hope this guide assists you in using your practice time more constructively and ignites renewed excitement in your playing.

—Luke Zecchin

Introduction

Jam tracks for guitar players aren't a new concept. The appeal is obvious. It's like having a backing band that fits into your pocket and doesn't mind listening to you solo for hours on end! Despite this, many don't think to use backing tracks as a regular practice tool or don't incorporate them as effectively as they could in their practice.

Sometimes, improving our skill at something isn't necessarily about the amount of time we spend; it's about how we spend our time. Practicing guitar in smaller *bite-sized* chunks can be a very effective way to concentrate on different elements of our playing. As guitarists, we tend to fall into the trap of playing a lot without really *practicing* anything. While mindless meandering around the fretboard isn't always a bad thing, it doesn't train us to be musical in our phrasing, expression, and feel.

Practicing in the context of a song forces us to think more about what we're playing. We have to listen to what we're doing to create something that sounds musically coherent. We don't just want to practice playing isolated licks and scales; we also want to practice *hearing* them in context. As such, jam tracks can help cultivate an awareness of what's happening around us when we play and train us to be sensitive to things like feel and timing. Developing solid rhythm and an ear for dynamics comes from playing with other musicians. Using high-quality backing tracks is a convenient way to simulate this experience.

The audio that accompanies this handbook aims to provide an engaging musical backdrop for practicing. (There's nothing less inspiring than jamming to something that sounds like it came pre-loaded on an old electric piano.) This collection of jam tracks draws on influences from rock, pop, blues, and folk. It was put together to span a number of key signatures, both major and minor. Although the songs aim to have a cohesive sound, they intentionally vary in feel and tempo. Experimenting with different keys and tempos ensures that we're continually widening our comfort zone on the fretboard.

As suggested in the book title, each backing track is approximately 5 minutes long. These short time frames accommodate using various songs within a single practice session. For example, if you have 25 minutes per day to practice, this time could be spent working through a handful of jam tracks. This would provide far more focus than just mindlessly noodling on autopilot for half an hour.

Not only is this a more constructive way to use your practice time, it also offers the added benefit of breaking down this time into smaller sections. These 5-minute chunks can be used much like timed training drills to concentrate on the specific areas of your playing that require attention.

Note: Before getting started, be sure to access your free online bonus material. To grab your jam tracks and bonus downloads, head to: **www.guitariq.com/5mj-bonus**

1

Structure & Mindset

Before looking at the specific jam tracks accompanying this handbook, let's discuss some general concepts for using backing tracks effectively in our practice time.

Thinking About Focus

When given the opportunity to play over a chord progression, the immediate temptation for many guitarists is to launch into an endless onslaught of scales and familiar licks. Although aimless noodling can be fun, constantly playing the same old things doesn't provide much opportunity to grow or challenge ourselves creatively. Again, while it may be difficult to practice without playing, it's very easy to play without really *practicing* anything.

One of the recurring concepts in this guide is simply that *focused practice is efficient practice*. This means being more intentional with your practice time. For example, when you sit down to play guitar, how often do you define the exact elements of your playing you're choosing to work on? Think about it. When was the last time you asked yourself: What are my exact objectives for the time I've dedicated to improve my playing today?

When we pick up the guitar, it's a fair assumption for most of us the goal is simply to practice. But practice what? What does that actually mean? Does it mean we're intending to work on our technique, our music theory, or our improvisation? Perhaps it means we want to improve our fretboard visualization, ear training, or songwriting skills? Most likely, it's a general combination of a number of these things, with no clear overall agenda.

Suppose we did actually predefine the focus of a practice session: *improvisation,* for example. What exact aspect of improvisation are we referring to? Do we want to work on our choice of melody and phrasing or our use of dynamics and emotion? Do we want to write some new melodic ideas or nail that difficult lick we can't quite play yet? Are we focused on our fretboard navigation skills or mastering a specific technique, and if so, which one?

While we could continue refining our focus even further, please don't confuse the point of this brief exercise. In truth, all these elements are connected. The intention isn't to overwhelm you with the many ways you could spend your practice time but to do precisely the opposite: to get you focused on the specifics of what you want to improve so your practice will be more effective.

Many guitar players experience the feeling of stunted creativity, like they're stuck playing the same old things and are unsure how to move forward. Identifying the particulars of what you want to improve sets a clear agenda for your practice time. A general desire to become a better guitar player is certainly positive, but it isn't overly *informative*. Articulating the specific skills or techniques you're looking to develop provides a clearer road map for achieving your goals.

> ***Tip:*** *Often, to move forward in your playing, it's helpful to think backward. Picture the overarching goal or skill set you'd like to achieve and then retrace the smaller steps required for getting there. While these steps will undoubtedly evolve as your knowledge increases, reflecting on this process will help provide clarity and direction for how you spend your practice time.*

Thinking About Structure

Having discussed being more intentional with your practice time, let's consider some specific suggestions for working with the jam tracks provided (or any backing tracks for that matter). Before sitting down to play guitar, think about the time you have and the number of songs you'd like to work through. This will be different for everybody. Some might spend 15 minutes warming up with practice tracks before focusing the rest of their time on learning a new song or, better yet, *writing* a new song. Others might prefer spending an hour or more working exclusively with the jam tracks. How you structure your time is up to you. The point here is to have some kind of *structure* in the first place. Below are some examples of how you might use jam tracks to focus on specific elements of your playing.

Scales

Scales are the building blocks for our melodic vocabulary. Backing tracks are a fantastic way to practice using them, because they add a lot more musicality to a task that can otherwise seem somewhat uninspiring. For those just starting out with scales, it may be helpful to spend an entire song simply looping through one scale shape at a time. You could then switch backing tracks and practice using that scale in a different key—or, alternatively, repeat the track and practice a different position of the same scale. Those a little more experienced could use jam tracks to practice navigating through every position of a scale up and down the entire fretboard in various keys. Always remember, scales don't always have to be played the same way. Try alternating the rhythm to complement the feel of each backing track.

Chords

Chords aren't just important for playing rhythm guitar! As a lead guitarist, having a thorough knowledge of the progression you're playing over is extremely valuable. Understanding the chords being used helps shape our melodic decisions. As chord charts are provided for each song, some may find it helpful to practice playing along, focusing on technique and timing. More advanced players could use the progressions provided and practice coming up with alternative chord voicings or inversions. Experiment with playing each progression in multiple ways, using various positions on the fretboard.

Arpeggios

Arpeggios are essentially *chord shapes* found within the different scales we're using. These shapes can be used melodically to accentuate the chord tones within a particular key. Using jam tracks, less experienced players can practice locating the arpeggio patterns found within the scales they're working on. More experienced players can use jam tracks to practice major and minor arpeggios in all positions on the fretboard at various tempos. Try altering these patterns to include a 7th or 9th for added color. As backing tracks often follow a consistent progression, they're also a fantastic way to practice *playing over the changes*. This means emphasizing the arpeggio shape that corresponds to each specific chord change when improvising over a piece of music.

Technique

Playing technique underpins everything we do on guitar. While *good* technique should be a focus regardless of what's being played, backing tracks can be used to work on specific areas of technique needing development. This applies to players of all skill levels. Perhaps your left hand needs to develop more strength in the little finger, or maybe your picking technique lacks accuracy and speed. It could be you just want to experiment with a skill you haven't mastered yet. Whatever the case, we can use jam tracks to create small training drills and then experiment with applying those exercises in different keys at various tempos. Try repeating the same track, each time focusing on a different element of your playing technique. Execution of fundamental skills such as the use of legato, vibrato, bends, and slides are all good examples of this.

Fretboard Navigation

Fretboard navigation is a fairly broad term. In many ways, it incorporates different elements from each of the previous examples. Simply put, backing tracks can help extend our use of fretboard real estate when playing in particular keys. This could involve navigating through scales and arpeggios in every position on the guitar neck, or learning how various scale patterns and chord shapes overlap one another in a single playing position. In either situation, *visualization* is an important concept. Being able to clearly visualize the way things are connected on the fretboard helps us apply this information with more fluency. Experiment with playing similar melodic ideas in different positions on the guitar neck. Focus on how the tone and feel changes even though the notes may stay the same.

Improvisation

Improvisation is more than making something up on the spot; it's about expressing yourself through your instrument. Jam tracks are obviously an essential tool for working on this ability. Use your practice time to break down the specifics of this skill. Repeat the same jam track several times, each time focusing on a different element of your playing. Use of dynamics, phrasing, and melody are all examples of this. Try experimenting with alternate scales or the use of *chromatic notes*. See if you can sing the melody you're playing, while you're playing it. Perhaps challenge yourself to use only two or three notes for an entire song. Maybe even limit yourself to playing on just one string. Often, mixing things up or working within self-imposed limitations helps us see things in a new way. As with all these examples, the secret to being creative is simply learning to *think creatively*!

The 5-Minute Mindset

Now that we've covered a number of suggestions for using jam tracks more productively, the real goal is to get you thinking for yourself. Other ways to structure your practice time might include the use of specific warm-up exercises, drills for developing speed, learning new licks to add to your musical vocabulary, and so on. There are no rules here! It's about experimentation and finding what works for you.

To clarify, please note that the concept here isn't to *only* practice certain skills in isolation. There's little point becoming proficient at playing particular scales or arpeggios if we don't practice using them in our improvisation or songwriting. Integrating different concepts and techniques is therefore extremely important. The end goal is for all elements of our playing to work together seamlessly. Becoming more deliberate with our practice time also doesn't mean there shouldn't be room for spontaneity in our practice structure. Spontaneity is an important part of creativity. The structures we create for ourselves exist to serve our creativity, not hinder it.

To reiterate, the central point is developing the ability to break things down into their smaller components in order to clearly define our focus. While this doesn't necessarily require the use of jam tracks, they not only offer a more musical context for practicing but also provide short, concentrated blocks in which to structure our time. Again, playing in context and thinking intentionally will help ensure we're maximizing our effort.

Ultimately, the idea of this *5-minute* mindset isn't really concerned with the actual number of minutes spent concentrating on any given task. It's about having a clear system for developing and reflecting on the various elements that contribute to our playing ability as a whole. This is the simple, yet powerful, premise behind **5-Minute Guitar Jams**.

Tip: Learning guitar isn't a sprint. Pace yourself. Don't become so overwhelmed with all the ways you could improve your playing that you end up working on none of them! Narrow your focus and concentrate on those things that align with your specific goals.

Tips for Improvisation

As one last stop before picking up the guitar, let's focus on some central insights concerning improvisation. The numerous benefits of incorporating jam tracks into our practice have already been outlined in this chapter. While backing tracks shouldn't be seen exclusively as a tool for improvising, improvisation does warrant special attention. Why? Because it provides a valuable critique on our playing as a whole. Improvisation requires that our playing technique, skills at fretboard navigation, and musical intuition all work together. It's also an immediate and effective way to experiment with new patterns, techniques, and concepts. Beyond this, most importantly, it's fun!

Improvisation, by its very nature, is defined by spontaneity; it's a free-form musical expression. As such, it's difficult to definitively outline a *correct* approach to improvising over a piece of music. Creativity, after all, is completely subjective! Having said that, if we're looking to craft solos that are just as enjoyable to listen to as they are to play, there are some fundamental concepts that recur across many genres and playing styles.

Improvisation, like all aspects of learning guitar, is a skill that needs to be practiced. Finding your own voice on the guitar requires learning how to speak the language of music fluently. As you work through these backing tracks, here are some key points worth considering:

- **Think Melody First:** A keen sense of melody is the difference between sounding like you're playing scales and sounding like you're playing *music*. Concentrating on melody brings focus to your musical ideas and creates a more engaging interaction with the listener.

- **Emotion Is Key:** The feel and emotion of *how* something is played say equally as much as what's played. Sometimes, simpler musical ideas played with feeling communicate significantly more than overly complex phrases, regardless of the technical proficiency they may require.

- **Focus on Dynamics:** Dynamics are a central channel through which feeling is conveyed. They encompass a wide range of sonic variances: loud, soft, simple, complex, tense, resolved, fast, and slow, for example. A dynamic performance will draw on various modes of expression.

- **Concentrate on Phrasing:** Melodic ideas should communicate something. Sensitivity to phrasing is what separates non-musical meanderings from coherent musical statements. Think about improvisation in terms of a *conversation*, where melodic statements are made and then responded to.

- **Make Use of Repetition:** Establishing, revisiting, and embellishing similar melodic themes throughout a song are key tools in songwriting. Not only does this type of repetition provide more mileage from a single melodic idea, but it also introduces structure and familiarity into a performance.

- **Be Sensitive to Space:** We often have a tendency to overplay, to fill up every space between phrases. This can confuse the main melodic ideas we're trying to express and become quite tiresome to listen to. Often, what you *don't* play says just as much as what you do play.

- **Technique Is a Tool:** Ultimately, technique should support musicality, not replace it. It's easy to develop an unbalanced fascination with speed and other technical aspects of guitar playing. While efficient and accurate technique is essential, it should never be the end goal itself.

- **Don't Ignore Theory:** While theory is no substitute for creativity, it provides the foundation for it. Understanding the essentials of how chords and scales are related will shape the essence of your musical vocabulary. Music theory informs and underpins everything we do on guitar.

- **Practice Creativity:** Creativity is a way of thinking. Train yourself to play with your *ears*, not your fingers. Our fingers always gravitate toward the familiar patterns and ideas they're used to playing. Try to practice hearing melodic ideas in your head before you play them on the fretboard.

- **Remember to Listen:** For a musician, *listening* is as important as playing. Music has an innate ability to tell you where it needs to go. Paying careful attention to the movement and instrumentation surrounding what you play will help ensure that a song sounds cohesive as a whole.

2

5-Minute Jams

Now that we've discussed some central concepts for working with backing tracks,
let's take an in-depth look at the jam tracks accompanying this guide.

Using This Handbook

In this chapter, we'll now shift focus from the conceptual to the practical. The following sections directly accompany the audio that's provided with this handbook. While much of this content will hopefully be self-explanatory, it may be helpful to briefly summarize the information provided.

This chapter outlines several chord progressions relating to specific key signatures. Basic track information is noted at the beginning of each section. This includes the key, time signature, and tempo of each jam track. In reference to the accompanying audio, the track number of each song is also provided.

The listed scales and arpeggios under *Primary Options* refer to popular patterns often used when playing over progressions in that key. The numbered sequences in the brackets alongside each suggestion (e.g., R - 3 - 5 - 7) refer to how that pattern relates to the structure of its parent major or minor scale. Below are examples of these patterns in the keys of C major and A minor.

Example 2.1

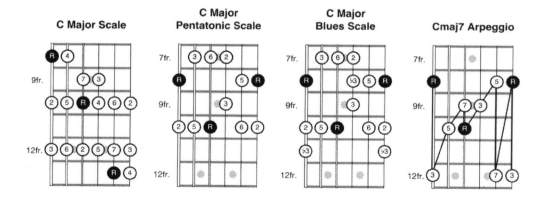

Example 2.2

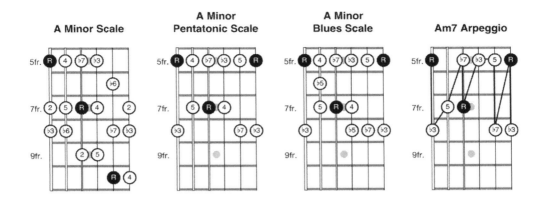

Tip: *These examples highlight how multiple patterns can be interchangeable within a single position on the fretboard. Although these shapes are a great starting point, it's important to remember that each scale and arpeggio pattern can be played in numerous ways across the guitar neck (please refer to* **Chapter 3***).*

The options under *Additional Suggestions* highlight a couple of other alternatives you could incorporate into your improvisation. While this isn't meant to be an exhaustive list, these represent some secondary options to experiment with. Typically, these patterns will sound less *resolved* than the primary ones, but they can be easily merged into melodic ideas for added interest and tonal character.

Importantly, the numbered sequences in brackets alongside these secondary suggestions (e.g., 3 - 5 - 7 - 9) refer to how each pattern relates to the specific key we might be playing over. In other words, these numbers highlight the *intervals* each pattern will accent in regards to the parent major or minor scale of the key. They don't refer to the internal structure of the specific pattern itself.

Note: Underlined numbers (e.g., R - 2 - b3 - 3 - 5 - 6) show those notes outside the diatonic structure of the key we're playing in. These chromatic notes are considered to be *passing tones* because they aren't found within the key center we're playing in.

Finally, neck diagrams and guitar TAB relating to each progression are also provided. For simplicity, the included TAB is a demonstration of the progression used, not a transcription of the entire jam track. For those working with the suggested audio accompaniment, these charts represent how each progression was recorded. Others preferring to use this handbook by itself can interpret information such as tempo and strumming patterns to taste.

Track List

Below you'll find a track list of each jam track provided:

1.   C Major Jam

2.   A Minor Jam

3.   A Major Jam

4.   F# Minor Jam

5.   G Major Jam

6.   E Minor Jam

7.   E Major Jam

8.   C# Minor Jam

9.   D Major Jam

10. B Minor Jam

C Major Jam

Track Information

- Track Number: 01

- Key Signature: C major

- Time Signature: 4 / 4

- Tempo: 85 BPM

Primary Options

- Cmaj7 arpeggio (R - 3 - 5 - 7)

- C major scale (R - 2 - 3 - 4 - 5 - 6 - 7)

- C major pentatonic scale (R - 2 - 3 - 5 - 6)

- C major blues scale (R - 2 - ♭3 - 3 - 5 - 6)

Additional Suggestions

- Em7 arpeggio (3 - 5 - 7 - 9)

- G major blues scale (5 - 6 - ♭7 - 7 - 2 - 3)

Chord Diagrams

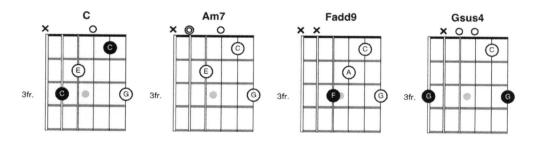

Chord Progression

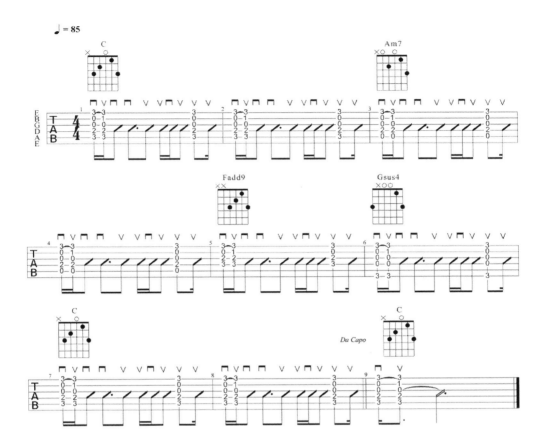

A Minor Jam

Track Information

- Track Number: 02

- Key Signature: A minor

- Time Signature: 4 / 4

- Tempo: 115 BPM

Primary Options

- Am7 arpeggio (R - ♭3 - 5 - ♭7)

- A minor scale (R - 2 - ♭3 - 4 - 5 - ♭6 - ♭7)

- A minor pentatonic scale (R - ♭3 - 4 - 5 - ♭7)

- A minor blues scale (R - ♭3 - 4 - ♭5 - 5 - ♭7)

Additional Suggestions

- Cmaj7 arpeggio (♭3 - 5 - ♭7 - 9)

- E minor blues scale (5 - ♭7 - R - ♭2 - 2 - 4)

Chord Diagrams

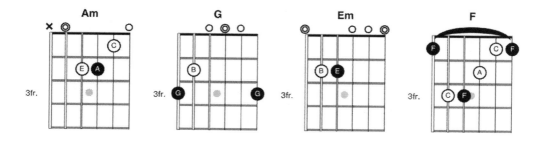

Chord Progression

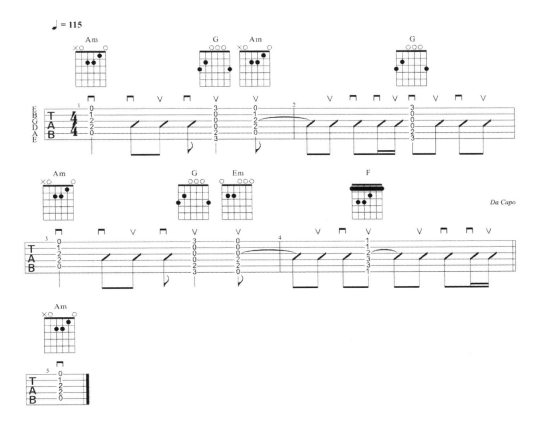

A Major Jam

Track Information

- Track Number: 03

- Key Signature: A major

- Time Signature: 4 / 4

- Tempo: 70 BPM

Primary Scales

- Amaj7 arpeggio (R - 3 - 5 - 7)

- A major scale (R - 2 - 3 - 4 - 5 - 6 - 7)

- A major pentatonic scale (R - 2 - 3 - 5 - 6)

- A major blues scale (R - 2 - ♭3 - 3 - 5 - 6)

Additional Suggestions

- C#m7 arpeggio (3 - 5 - 7 - 9)

- E major blues scale (5 - 6 - ♭7 - 7 - 2 - 3)

Chord Diagrams

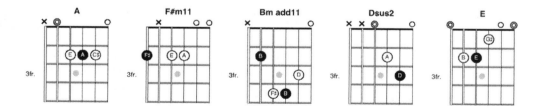

Chord Progression

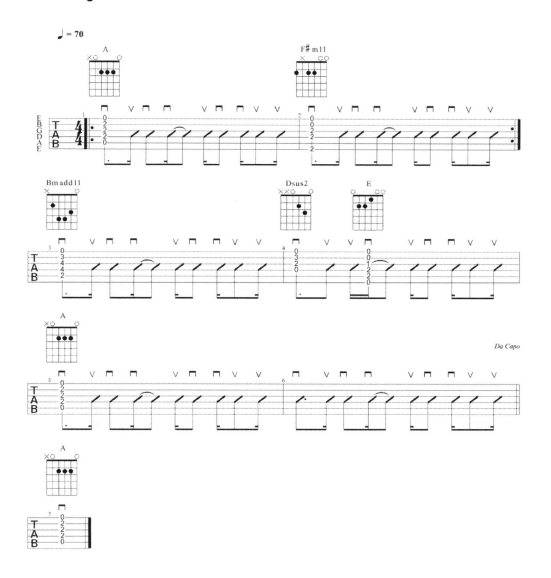

F# Minor Jam

Track Information

- Track Number: 04

- Key Signature: F# minor

- Time Signature: 6 / 8

- Tempo: 100 BPM

Primary Options

- F#m7 arpeggio (R - ♭3 - 5 - ♭7)

- F# minor scale (R - 2 - ♭3 - 4 - 5 - ♭6 - ♭7)

- F# minor pentatonic scale (R - ♭3 - 4 - 5 - ♭7)

- F# minor blues scale (R - ♭3 - 4 - <u>♭5</u> - 5 - ♭7)

Additional Suggestions

- Amaj7 arpeggio (♭3 - 5 - ♭7 - 9)

- C# minor blues scale (5 - ♭7 - R - <u>♭2</u> - 2 - 4)

Chord Diagrams

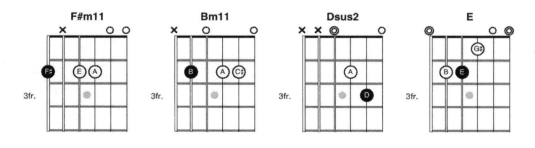

Chord Progression

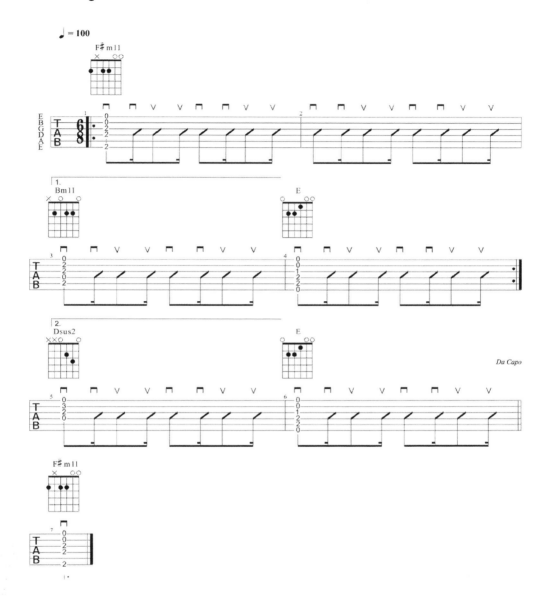

G Major Jam

Track Information

- Track Number: 05

- Key Signature: G major

- Time Signature: 4 / 4

- Tempo: 80 BPM

Primary Options

- Gmaj7 arpeggio (R - 3 - 5 - 7)

- G major scale (R - 2 - 3 - 4 - 5 - 6 - 7)

- G major pentatonic scale (R - 2 - 3 - 5 - 6)

- G major blues scale (R - 2 - ♭3 - 3 - 5 - 6)

Additional Suggestions

- Bm7 arpeggio (3 - 5 - 7 - 9)

- D major blues scale (5 - 6 - ♭7 - 7 - 2 - 3)

Chord Diagrams

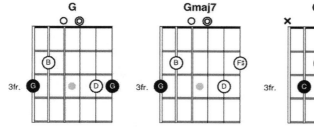
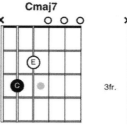
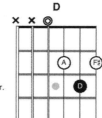

Chord Progression

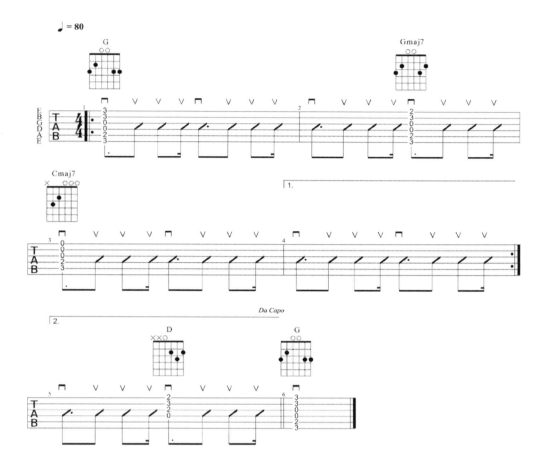

E Minor Jam

Track Information

- Track Number: 06

- Key Signature: E minor

- Time Signature: 4 / 4

- Tempo: 90 BPM

Primary Options

- Em7 arpeggio (R - ♭3 - 5 - ♭7)

- E minor scale (R - 2 - ♭3 - 4 - 5 - ♭6 - ♭7)

- E minor pentatonic scale (R - ♭3 - 4 - 5 - ♭7)

- E minor blues scale (R - ♭3 - 4 - ♭5 - 5 - ♭7)

Additional Suggestions

- Gmaj7 arpeggio (♭3 - 5 - ♭7 - 9)

- B minor blues scale (5 - ♭7 - R - ♭2 - 2 - 4)

Chord Diagrams

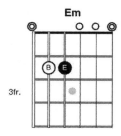
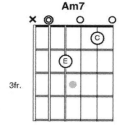
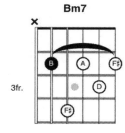

Chord Progression

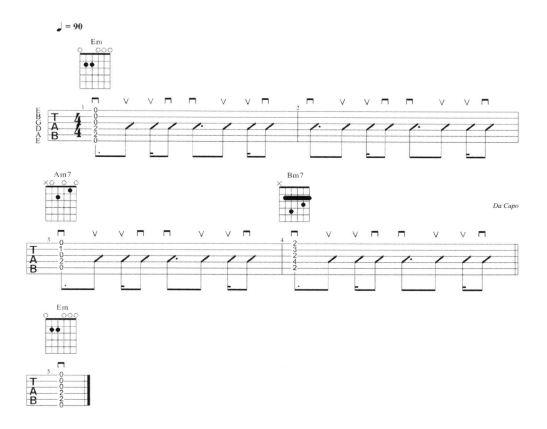

E Major Jam

Track Information

- Track Number: 07

- Key Signature: E major

- Time Signature: 4 / 4

- Tempo: 95 BPM

Primary Options

- Emaj7 arpeggio (R - 3 - 5 - 7)

- E major scale (R - 2 - 3 - 4 - 5 - 6 - 7)

- E major pentatonic scale (R - 2 - 3 - 5 - 6)

- E major blues scale (R - 2 - ♭3 - 3 - 5 - 6)

Additional Suggestions

- G#m7 arpeggio (3 - 5 - 7 - 9)

- B major blues scale (5 - 6 - ♭7 - 7 - 2 - 3)

Chord Diagrams

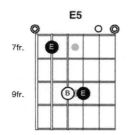

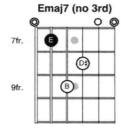

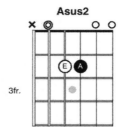

Chord Progression

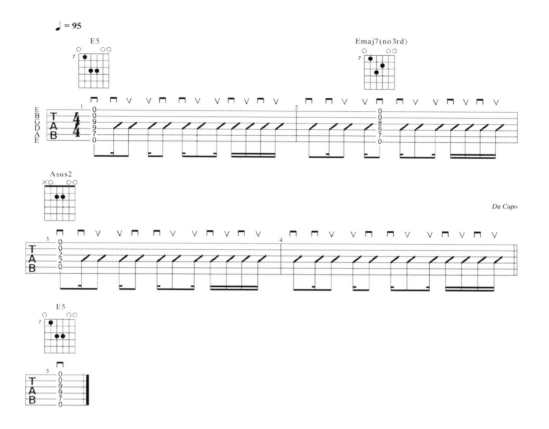

C# Minor Jam

Track Information

- Track Number: 08

- Key Signature: C# minor

- Time Signature: 4 / 4

- Tempo: 105 BPM

Primary Options

- C#m7 arpeggio (R - ♭3 - 5 - ♭7)

- C# minor scale (R - 2 - ♭3 - 4 - 5 - ♭6 - ♭7)

- C# minor pentatonic scale (R - ♭3 - 4 - 5 - ♭7)

- C# minor blues scale (R - ♭3 - 4 - ♭5 - 5 - ♭7)

Additional Suggestions

- Emaj7 arpeggio (♭3 - 5 - ♭7 - 9)

- G# minor blues scale (5 - ♭7 - R - ♭2 - 2 - 4)

Chord Diagrams

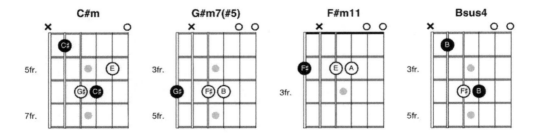

Chord Progression

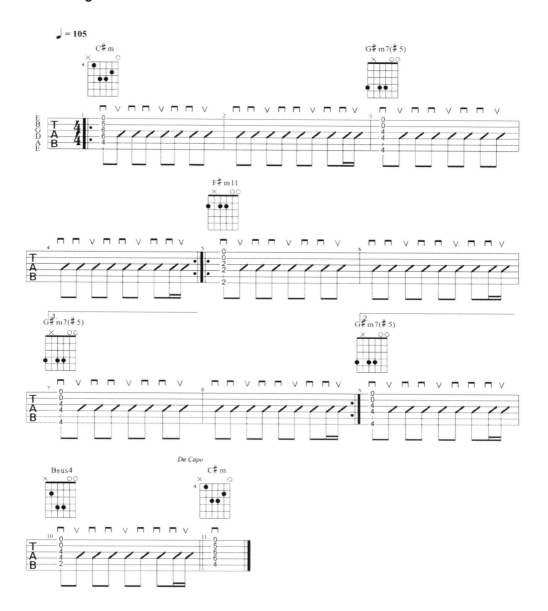

D Major Jam

Track Information

- Track Number: 09

- Key Signature: D major

- Time Signature: 4 / 4

- Tempo: 110 BPM

Primary Options

- Dmaj7 arpeggio (R - 3 - 5 - 7)

- D major scale (R - 2 - 3 - 4 - 5 - 6 - 7)

- D major pentatonic scale (R - 2 - 3 - 5 - 6)

- D major blues scale (R - 2 - ♭3 - 3 - 5 - 6)

Additional Suggestions

- F#m7 arpeggio (3 - 5 - 7 - 9)

- A major blues scale (5 - 6 - ♭7 - 7 - 2 - 3)

Chord Diagrams

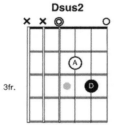
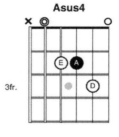
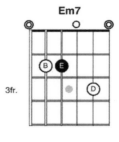
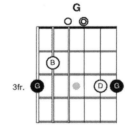

Chord Progression

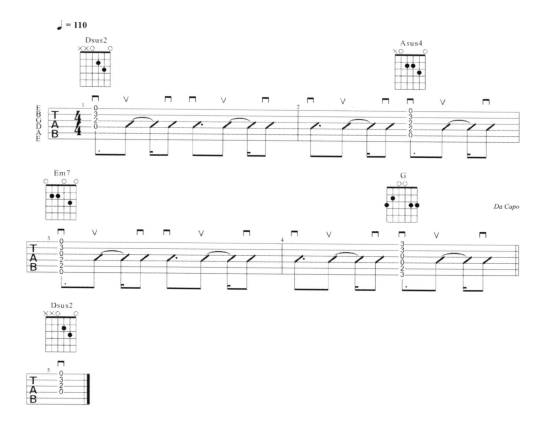

B Minor Jam

Track Information

- Track Number: 10

- Key Signature: B minor

- Time Signature: 4 / 4

- Tempo: 75 BPM

Primary Options

- Bm7 arpeggio (R - ♭3 - 5 - ♭7)

- B minor scale (R - 2 - ♭3 - 4 - 5 - ♭6 - ♭7)

- B minor pentatonic scale (R - ♭3 - 4 - 5 - ♭7)

- B minor blues scale (R - ♭3 - 4 - ♭5 - 5 - ♭7)

Additional Suggestions

- Dmaj7 arpeggio (♭3 - 5 - ♭7 - 9)

- F# minor blues scale (5 - ♭7 - R - ♭2 - 2 - 4)

Chord Diagrams

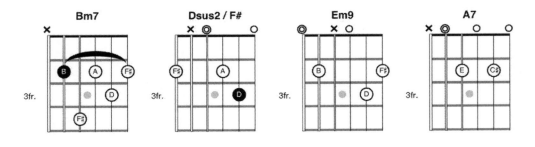

Chord Progression

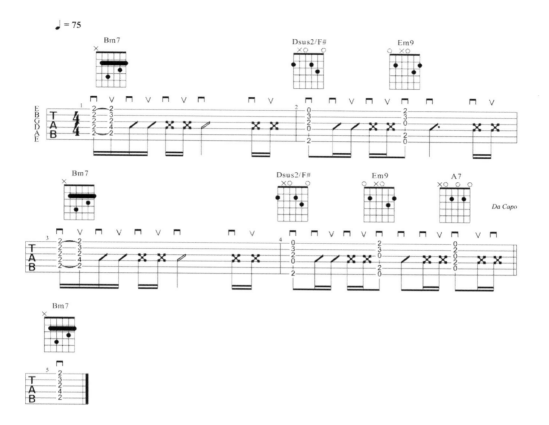

3

Quick Navigation Guide

Having referenced various scale shapes and arpeggio patterns, we'll now briefly explore how these options relate to the fretboard.

Visualizing Scales

The previous chapter took an in-depth look at the jam tracks accompanying this handbook. A lot of information was covered here, including numerous scale and arpeggio suggestions. While this handbook isn't intended to be a comprehensive guide for using scales, it seems fitting to conclude with demonstrating the key shapes and positions that have been discussed.

Throughout this guide, we've referred to four main pattern types for the purpose of improvisation. Again, these suggestions don't include all the options available to us when improvising or songwriting, but they do represent foundational patterns that span numerous genres. To reiterate, these are:

- major/minor scales

- major/minor pentatonic scales

- major/minor blues scales

- major/minor seventh arpeggios

In the following sections, we'll demonstrate what each pattern looks like in their various positions on the fretboard. Rather than outlining each shape in isolation, the intention is to show how they relate to one another. As such, the following diagrams are grouped not by their type but by their relative *position* on the fretboard.

Because pentatonic scales are a familiar starting point for many guitar players, we'll use the five positions of the pentatonic scale to reference our relative position on the fretboard. Notice the unique shapes created by the root notes in each set of patterns. Even though the shape of each pattern changes, the structure of the root notes does not. Practice using these *octave shapes* to reference the scales and arpeggios that are connected to them. (This concept is often referenced as part of the CAGED system.)

Lastly, these patterns are all *movable* shapes. While we'll be using the keys of C major and A minor for the following examples, these patterns can be applied to any key. If we're playing in B minor, for example, each A minor pattern would simply shift up a whole step.

Note: This chapter is intended to be a quick reference guide for visualizing the various patterns that have been discussed. For more comprehensive lessons on fretboard navigation, theory, and technique please refer to my book **Lead Guitar Breakthrough**.

Major Scales & Arpeggios

Example 3.1

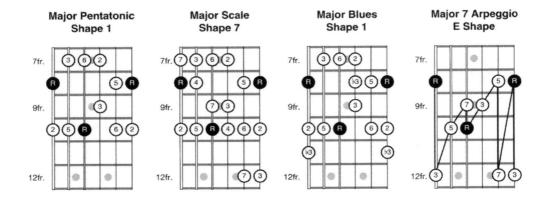

Example 3.2

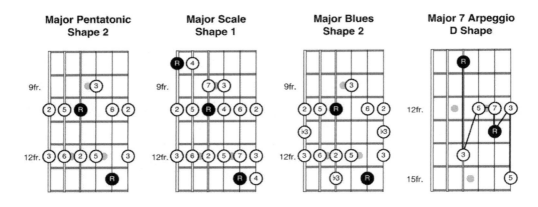

Example 3.3

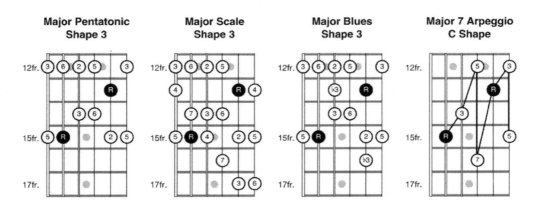

Example 3.4

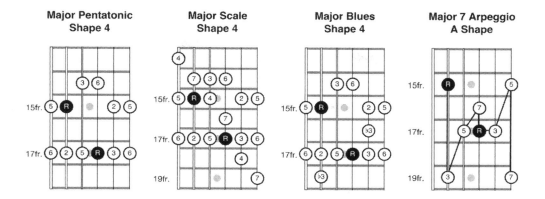

Major Pentatonic Shape 4 · Major Scale Shape 4 · Major Blues Shape 4 · Major 7 Arpeggio A Shape

Example 3.5

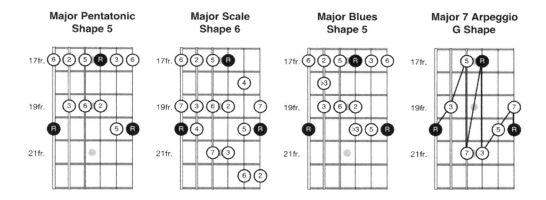

Major Pentatonic Shape 5 · Major Scale Shape 6 · Major Blues Shape 5 · Major 7 Arpeggio G Shape

Minor Scales & Arpeggios

Example 3.6

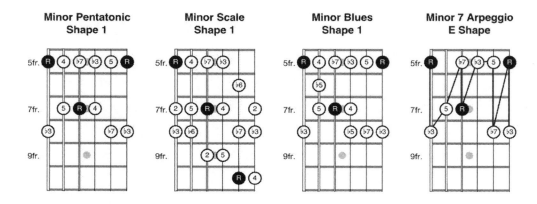

Example 3.7

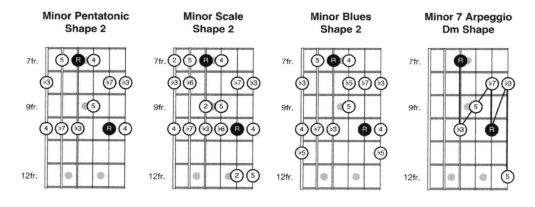

Example 3.8

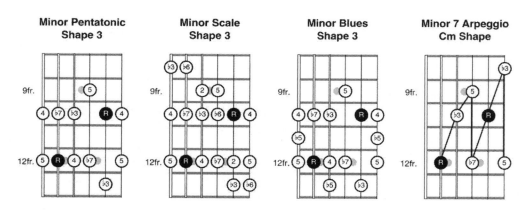

Example 3.9

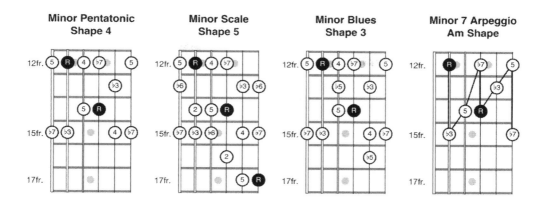

Minor Pentatonic Shape 4 · Minor Scale Shape 5 · Minor Blues Shape 3 · Minor 7 Arpeggio Am Shape

Example 3.10

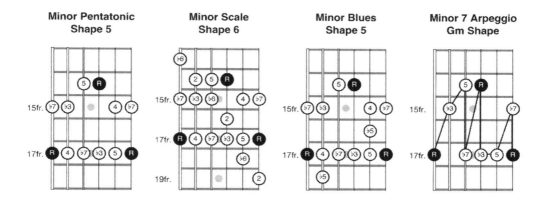

Minor Pentatonic Shape 5 · Minor Scale Shape 6 · Minor Blues Shape 5 · Minor 7 Arpeggio Gm Shape

Final Thoughts

Congratulations on completing *5-Minute Guitar Jams*!

This handbook was written as a companion to those looking for a greater sense of motivation and direction in their practice time. Throughout this guide, we've focused on two key concepts: playing *in context* and practicing with *intention*. Accordingly, jam tracks have been emphasized repeatedly as an effective method for promoting both ideas.

To summarize, practicing in the context of a song places our playing pursuits, both creative and technical, into a more realistic musical environment. We're forced to experiment with various keys and tempos, listen in greater detail to what we're playing, and be sensitive to the instrumentation around us. Practicing in repetitive bite-sized chunks allows us to narrow down our focus to the particular elements of our playing we're looking to improve. In this way, being intentional with our focus maximizes the effectiveness of our time and effort.

It's been the goal of this handbook not only to provide helpful material to use when practicing but, more importantly, to offer a fresh way of thinking about practicing. Sometimes, even small adjustments can produce big results. I hope this simple guide will be a valuable reference as you continue to work through both the jam tracks provided and the future practice material you'll encounter.

May this book help inspire you toward continued learning and creativity.

Additional Resources

For more resources, including great free content, be sure to visit us at:

www.guitariq.com

Stay in touch with all the latest news. To connect with us online, head to:

www.guitariq.com/connect

Would you like to read more? For a complete list of Luke's books, check out:

www.guitariq.com/books

Remember to grab your online bonus! Get the free bonus content for this book at:

www.guitariq.com/5mj-bonus

Interested in a master class with Luke? To check out his online workshops, go to:

www.guitariq.com/academy

About the Author

Having played for over 25 years, Luke Zecchin is an accomplished guitarist with a wealth of studio and live experience. Outside his work teaching music, Luke has toured extensively alongside renowned national and international acts, performing at everything from clubs, theaters, and festivals to various appearances on commercial radio and national television.

Playing lead guitar, Luke has worked on projects with established international producers and engineers. He has been fortunate to see these collaborations break into both the Top 50 ARIA Album and Singles charts, having also received nationwide airplay and notable debuts on the Australian iTunes Rock charts.

As the founder of **GuitarIQ.com**, Luke is dedicated to the education and coaching of guitar players all over the globe. With books available in over 100 countries worldwide, he has emerged as an international chart-topping author in his field.

Luke continues to work as an author and musician from his project studio based in the Adelaide Hills, South Australia.

Find him online at **LukeZecchin.com**.

Liked This Book?

Did you find this book useful? You can make a big difference in helping us spread the word!

While it would be nice to have the promotional muscle of a major publishing house, independent authors rely heavily on the loyalty of their audience. Online reviews are one of the most powerful tools we have for getting attention and finding new readers.

If you found this book helpful, please consider helping us by leaving an online review at your place of purchase. Reviews needn't be long or in-depth; a star rating with a short comment is perfect. If you could take a minute to leave your feedback, it would be sincerely appreciated!

38407925R00033

Printed in Great Britain
by Amazon